Greg Brown has been involved in sports for thirty years as an athlete and award-winning sportswriter. Brown started his Positively For Kids series after he was unable to find sports books that taught life lessons for his own children. Eric's book is the 17th in the series. Brown regularly speaks at schools and may be reached at greg@PositivelyForKids.com. He lives in Bothell, Washington, with his wife, Stacy, and two children, Lauren and Benji.

Doug Keith has provided illustrations for national magazines such as *Sports Illustrated for Kids*, greeting cards, and books. Keith may be reached at his internet address: atozdk@aol.com.

All photos courtesy of Eric Lindros and family except the following:
AP/Wide World: 6, 38, 40 right. Bruce Bennett Studios: 4, 5, 25, 28, 30 top and right, 31, 32, 35, 39 left, 40 left. Children's Miracle Network: 3 right, 37. *Sports Illustrated*: 27 left, 32 right, 33, 34 bottom left.
Information on Canadians in pro hockey on page 15 from "Straight Facts on Making It in Pro Hockey," at www.omha.net/admin/012199_parcels.html

Eric Lindros will donate all royalties from the sale of this book to the Children's Miracle Network.
To learn more about Eric Lindros and his work with the Children's Miracle Network, go to: **www.ericlindros.net**.

Published by Taylor Publishing Company
1550 West Mockingbird Lane
Dallas, Texas 75235
www.taylorpub.com

Designed by Steve Willgren

Library of Congress Cataloging-in-Publication Data
Lindros, Eric.
    Pursue your goals / by Eric Lindros with Greg Brown ; illustrations by Doug Keith
        p.   cm.
    ISBN 0-87833-167-0
    1. Lindros, Eric. 2. Hockey players—Canada—Biography—Juvenile literature. I. Brown, Greg. II. Keith, Doug, ill. III. Title.
    GV848.5.L56 A35 1999
                                                99-054410

Printed in the United States of America

10 9 8 7 6 5 4 3 2 1

PURSUE YOUR GOALS

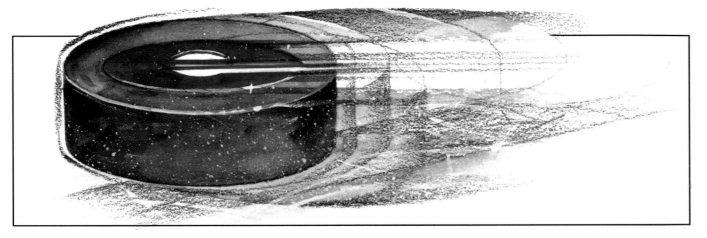

by Eric Lindros

with Greg Brown

Illustrations by Doug Keith

Taylor Publishing Company

Dallas, Texas

PURSUE YOUR GOALS

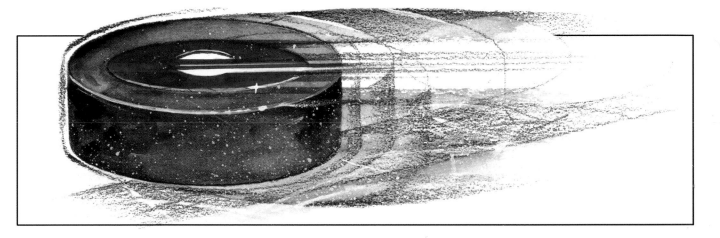

by Eric Lindros

with Greg Brown
Illustrations by Doug Keith

Taylor Publishing Company

Dallas, Texas

Greg Brown has been involved in sports for thirty years as an athlete and award-winning sportswriter. Brown started his Positively For Kids series after he was unable to find sports books that taught life lessons for his own children. Eric's book is the 17th in the series. Brown regularly speaks at schools and may be reached at greg@PositivelyForKids.com. He lives in Bothell, Washington, with his wife, Stacy, and two children, Lauren and Benji.

Doug Keith has provided illustrations for national magazines such as *Sports Illustrated for Kids*, greeting cards, and books. Keith may be reached at his internet address: atozdk@aol.com.

Eric Lindros will donate all royalties from the sale of this book to the Children's Miracle Network.
To learn more about Eric Lindros and his work with the Children's Miracle Network, go to:
www.ericlindros.net.

All photos courtesy of Eric Lindros and family except the following:
AP/Wide World: 6, 38, 40 right. Bruce Bennett Studios: 4, 5, 25, 28, 30 top and right, 31, 32, 35, 39 left, 40 left. Children's Miracle Network: 3 right, 37. *Sports Illustrated*: 27 left, 32 right, 33, 34 bottom left.
Information on Canadians in pro hockey on page 15 from "Straight Facts on Making It in Pro Hockey," at www.omha.net/admin/012199_parcels.html

Published by Taylor Publishing Company
1550 West Mockingbird Lane
Dallas, Texas 75235
www.taylorpub.com

Designed by Steve Willgren

Library of Congress Cataloging-in-Publication Data
Lindros, Eric.
    Pursue your goals / by Eric Lindros with Greg Brown ; illustrations by Doug Keith
        p.   cm.
    ISBN 0-87833-167-0
    1. Lindros, Eric. 2. Hockey players—Canada—Biography—Juvenile literature. I. Brown, Greg. II. Keith, Doug, ill. III. Title.
    GV848.5.L56 A35 1999
                                          99-054410

Printed in the United States of America

10   9   8   7   6   5   4   3   2   1

My first grade picture.

Hi. I'm Eric Lindros. I play hockey for a living. Because of my six-foot-four, 235-pound size and skating speed, some people call me the "E-Train." Friends and family just call me "E." Others call me the ultimate power forward, combining scoring and passing skills with a willingness to play a physical game.

I have experienced many things at an early age, thanks to hockey. I was the youngest ever to play in the Canada Cup at age eighteen. The first name picked in the 1991 National Hockey League draft was mine. I've played in two Olympics, winning silver in '92. I've been honored as the Most Valuable Player of the NHL, and know the exhilaration of playing in the Stanley Cup Finals.

My journey, however, has not been smooth as a sheet of ice. I've had my ups and downs, like everyone else.

Through it all, I've learned a few things I want to share with you in this book. One of the most important is this: To go anywhere, to be anything, it takes more than just having dreams. You must be willing to pursue your goals.

To me, the first thing you need to achieve any goal is a positive outlook—be willing and eager to discover what's around the corner on life's road. Along the way, there will be obstacles. But you have to believe there are no dead ends, just bumps and curves.

At every level of hockey, from my first year to the NHL, I've faced many challenges.

I've been willing to test myself at every level to see how far I could go. Once you have a positive outlook, you have to be willing to try. It's all about the pursuit.

In addition to trying hard, athletes need a competitive fire to go the extra mile. The emotion comes from doing something you love.

I've played other team sports, including baseball and soccer. But hockey is my first love.

Hockey brings out the best, and sometimes the worst, in people. Yes, hockey can be rough, but so can life. Some say life is like hockey. In Canada, where I grew up, hockey is life.

While hockey is important, it is not my whole life. Hockey taught me that at the end of the 1998–99 season.

It happened in Nashville, Tennessee, during a regular-season NHL game between the Predators and the Philadelphia Flyers on April 1, 1999—and this was no April Fool's joke.

I believe it happened in the first period after a cross-check when I fell on a hockey stick. The blade curled up under my ribs as I landed hard on it. I thought I had broken a couple of ribs.

I told our Flyer trainer about my pain, but decided to keep playing. Shortly after the game, every breath, every movement, caused bolts of pain. Back at the team hotel, laying in bed made breathing worse, so I slipped into a hot bath, thinking that might ease my discomfort. I now realize by sitting upright in the tub I was able to breathe more freely.

During the night, Keith Jones, my teammate and roommate, checked on me. He found me in agony in the tub. Finally, at Keith's insistance, an ambulance was called shortly after 9 A.M. and it rushed me to a hospital emergency room.

Doctors discovered a badly bruised lung and half my blood supply leaking into my chest cavity, causing one lung to collapse. Immediate surgery in the emergency room saved my life.

Brett, my brother, heard the news and flew down to see me immediately. Tubes going in and out of me made me look like an octopus of hoses.

Brothers don't always need to speak words. His being there was enough.

Brett and I have a special bond, thanks to hockey. We dreamed of playing hockey on the same team, but it never happened. A series of concussions cut short Brett's professional hockey career three and a half years earlier. My parents came down from Toronto to be with me, too. I spent nearly two weeks in the hospital and needed two operations.

If hockey has taught me anything, it's that family comes first. During times when it seemed everyone was against me, my family always has been there with their loving support. All the way from the beginning . . .

I was born February 28, 1973, in London, Ontario, a town about 120 miles from Toronto.

Both my parents came from sports-minded families and both were athletes themselves. Bonnie, my mom, almost six feet tall, played basketball and competed in track and field during high school. She anchored a relay team that set a county record. My parents first met at a high school track meet in their hometown of Chatham, Ontario.

Carl, my dad, who stands six-foot-five, played basketball, football, and hockey. He made the Chicago Black Hawks junior farm team, but he chose to walk away because the coaches only wanted him to be a goon on the ice and start fights.

Instead, Dad played college football at the University of Western Ontario and was drafted by the Edmonton Eskimos of the Canadian Football League. Dad, however, decided to start his business life rather than play pro football. He graduated from the University's business school and became a successful public accountant. Mom became a registered nurse.

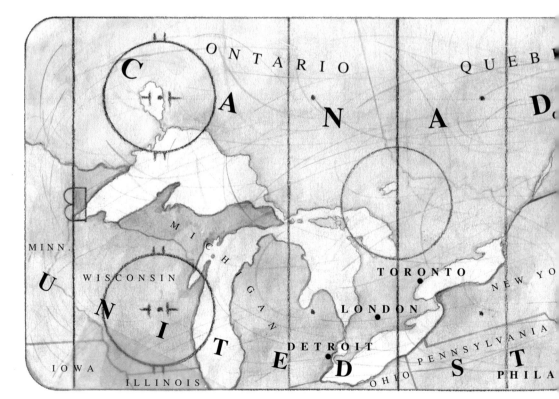

Because I was the first of three children in our family, my parents didn't know much about parenting when I came along.

There are parenting classes out there, but most parents learn on the job. So when I showed early signs of coordination, such as walking at seven and a half months, they didn't think anything of it. And like most Canadians, my parents strapped double-bladed skates on me as soon as I could stand.

They thought my large hands were perfectly normal. From just about the beginning, however, they knew my energy level was off the scale.

This is how big my hand was when I was just seven and a half years old.

9

This photo catches me pinching Mom.

Mom had to keep her eye on me constantly. As a toddler, I grew into a whirlwind of motion. I could get into trouble in the time it took her to turn her head.

For example, at eighteen months old, I woke up early one morning and tried my hand at cooking. While standing on a chair, I moved the electrical heating elements to the top of the stove and turned them on. Mom awoke to scraping metal sounds. When she got to the kitchen, I stood proudly in my yellow blanket sleeper, stirring the stove with a wooden spoon—a burning wooden spoon! Mom saved me and asked what I was doing. I calmly said, "I cooking."

One time, I tore down our dining room curtain when I played toddler Tarzan to get Mom's atttention so she'd get off the phone. It worked.

I drove my parents crazy. When Brett was born, nearly three years after me, we created double trouble.

Me and Brett.

I frightened my parents many times by being a daredevil. I would sled down snow-covered hills and run smack into snow banks, just to see what it felt like. (I don't recommend you try it.)

I'd race around on our sidewalk on a bicycle without training wheels (which I could ride before I turned three), narrowly missing things and people.

My most memorable scare as a child happened at London's Storybook Gardens when I was about two and a half. I remember looking over a fence to get a close-up view of a peacock.

The colorful bird took one look at me and charged, with an ear-piercing squawk and feathers flying. I staggered away from the fence in shock, crying.

Speaking of fears, I've never been able to enjoy horror movies. Even today, when I watch one I have to keep telling myself over and over, "This isn't real, this isn't real."

My biggest fear growing up was the possibility of losing a parent. The father of a friend of mine died at a young age. I worried about that happening to our family, which is one reason I wanted to stay close to home during my teen years.

Whether I was on a tire swing, building a snow fort, or fishing, I loved playing outside. Indoors, any type of game I played brought out my competitive spirit.

Mom signed me up for the scouts program to keep me busy. I started as a "Beaver." Because of my advanced hand-eye coordination, I enjoyed sewing. I'm not embarrassed to say that I took pride in making place mats in seventh grade for a class project, which earned an A grade.

My first day of kindergarten.

My parents always stressed the importance of taking pride in schoolwork. They had seen how those who are educated create more choices for themselves. Those who learn needed skills through education have more personal freedom to choose where and how they live and work. Pro hockey has interrupted my college studies, but I plan on getting my degree someday.

My first day at college.

My first day of kindergarten gave my mother great relief (by getting a break from me), and my first day of college gave both my parents great pride.

School wasn't that tough for me, as long as I used my time wisely. At the Lindros house, we were expected to do our best, and I did. We couldn't play pickup hockey or goof around after school until our homework was complete.

My parents didn't have grand visions of the NHL when they signed up their six-year-old son for his first hockey team in the Red Circle league. I certainly didn't think of being an NHL player.

I started hockey in a non-contact league. Mom hoped it would burn off my excess energy. It sure did. And hockey hooked me. I thrived on the games, even though I wasn't the best player.

But a family problem developed. During our drive home after games, Dad would go over every mistake I made on the ice. Mom noticed how my excitement for hockey burst once I got in the car with Dad.

For a while, driving two cars to my games became our solution. Dad would drive home by himself.

To his credit, Dad went the extra mile to talk with experts in coaching kids. He discovered that parental criticism often crushes a young athlete's love of sports. He learned that the best thing parents can do after games is to comment on the positive plays their child made and to show their unconditional support, win or lose. Dad learned that lesson well.

Dad also taught me about practicing and having fun.

He became a master at building backyard ice rinks in the winter. He would flood our backyard grass when temperatures dipped below freezing.

He fussed over making it perfect. As spring approached, he'd drive to the local artificial rink and fill our station wagon with excess snow from the Zamboni (an ice-cleaning machine) to patch our ice.

We were so into our rink that in the third grade I did a class project on the best method of making a backyard rink. When we moved to Toronto our backyard had a pool, but Dad destroyed it. He filled the hole with dirt and planted grass on top so we would have a winter rink.

After hockey games, I'd go out on our rink by myself and replay every situation under the moonlight. Mom would call me to come in, and I'd beg for just "five more minutes." I couldn't get enough ice time. To me, it was heaven.

Our rink became a neighborhood focal point for some shinny (a Canadian term for pickup games). Our "friendly" games gave us kids extra time to practice our hockey skills while having fun.

After Dad got home from work, he often showed me a few drills to work on. I practiced backhands and slapshots, passing and skating drills. He'd always make a game of it. Sometimes the whole family would be on the ice.

Because our rink wasn't that big and was subject to thawing weather, sometimes Dad and I would get up early and sneak onto the public outdoor artificial rinks before they opened. My game quickly improved as we worked on my strengths and weaknesses.

My parents strongly believe that kids shouldn't play the same sport year round. So after the winter hockey season, I'd play a different sport or take a break. My parents said we needed "down time" to be kids. I think it worked out for the best.

I still thought about hockey in the summer. When September came, I'd start shooting off a hard piece of plastic in our backyard or go to my Dad's office and shoot pucks in the parking lot. To me, practicing hockey wasn't work. I loved it.

I can't say the same thing about the trumpet. I learned to play the trumpet in elementary school. At times, I pushed myself to become "first chair" in the band. But deep down my passion for the trumpet didn't compare to my passion for hockey.

I didn't always want to play my trumpet. One time, I recorded one of my practice sessions and then played it in my room so my parents thought I was practicing. That fooled them a few times, until Mom caught me.

Brett and me.

I felt caught between groups at school. I was quiet and somewhat shy.

I never felt I fit among the "in" group. I had friends, but was never the most popular. I didn't drink alcohol or try illegal drugs. I had a few girlfriends and experienced the heartache of being dumped. Hockey, however, was my main focus.

I'm not saying I was a saint, but I stayed out of trouble. Brett and I had our share of sibling spats, and sometimes our roughhousing broke things around the house. Mom usually punished us by making us clean the house, including toilets.

I did break a glass door once at school. It happened during a year I grew seven inches.

During those growth spurts, my coordination went haywire for a while. One day I reached to grab a school door handle and accidentally punched my fist through the door's glass.

20

I grew so fast, some seasons I'd go through three pairs of skates—at more than $100 a pair, that added up. So we'd try to squeeze as much time out of each pair. We'd buy them a size too big and stuff paper in the toes. To extend the fit, I skated without socks for several weeks before going to the next pair. Today, I prefer skating without socks.

Due to the width of my feet, I needed custom skates made by Bauer. One day I went in for foot measurements, even though I was sick. Dad and I stopped for a hamburger on the way.

Just before we arrived, I threw up all over my feet in the car. We didn't have any towels, so I wiped them in the grass before going in. The person measuring my feet must have thought I had a terrible foot odor problem.

At the start of one season, I desperately needed new skates. The company mailed the skates, but they didn't arrive on the first day of practice. Dad drove to the post office and helped go through piles of boxes until he found the skates—just in time. Like all loving parents, mine were willing to help their children pursue goals.

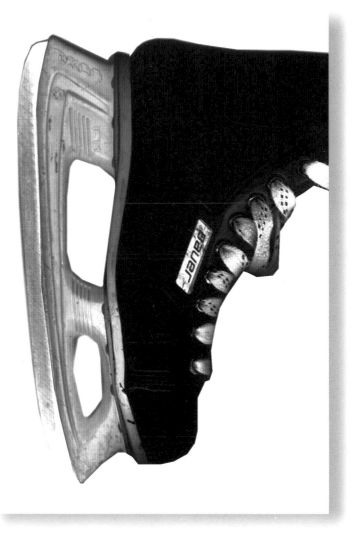

My parents reminded me about manners when we were eating at the homes of friends or family. During one such dinner, I patiently watched a huge bowl of potatoes make its way around the table. I then asked if anyone wanted more potatoes. When nobody said anything, I dumped the whole bowl on my plate.

I once almost burned out a toaster when I toasted and ate a whole loaf of raisin bread in one sitting.

Besides being known for hockey, I became known at school for my eating habits. Mom packed my school lunches in plastic grocery bags because paper bags would tear. A typical school lunch consisted of five peanut-butter-and-jam sandwiches, two fruits, cookies, celery sticks with peanut butter, and two juice boxes.

I forgot my lunch one day in elementary school. Mom brought it to class and handed it to my teacher, who asked if I was going to share it with the whole class or send it to the Third World.

In Toronto, you could try out for about eight teams each season. My parents never cared about whether I played on the best team or not. They cared more about kids developing skills and sportsmanship and having fun. They cared about the pursuit.

So when my parents saw a club coach of mine play most of a tournament game without a goalie to humiliate a weaker opponent, they made sure I played for a different coach the next season.

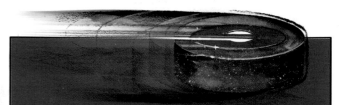

I had many great coaches throughout youth hockey who encouraged me. One coach, John Futa, handed out this poem to all his players when I was eleven, playing for the Toronto Marlboros. I carried the poem to every game as a kid. It took me years to realize these truths.

If you think you are beaten, you are
If you think you dare not, you don't
If you like to win, but think you can't,
It's almost certain you won't.
If you think you'll lose, you're lost.
For out of the world we find
Success begins with a fellow's will—
It's all in a state of mind.
If you think you're outclassed, you are
You've got to think high to rise.
You've got to be sure of yourself before
You can win the prize.
Life's battles don't always go
To the stronger or faster man.
But sooner or later, the man who wins
Is the man who thinks he CAN.

Some people didn't like our decision to switch teams. One day, when I was thirteen, I received a letter. When you're that age, any letter you get is usually a card or a gift from a relative. Naturally, I was excited. I opened it and read a hateful poem— from an adult. It said terrible things that shook me up. It said I'd never make it in hockey.

For months, before the hate mail finally stopped, my parents raced to beat me home from school to go through the day's mail.

My grade 6 school team.

23

John McCauley

As my skill level advanced beyond my years, I started practicing with older players at St. Mike's High School, about twenty-five blocks from our house. After school, I'd practice against the big boys.

At thirteen, I practiced against guys three to six years older, and held my own. The older players often teased me about the bike I rode to practice. Mom's blue bike, with a wicker front basket, was the only bike I had because mine was stolen at school. I wanted the extra practice so much, I rode the girls' bike and laughed off the jokes.

I played for St. Mike's, which has a long winning tradition, the next year. My development continued.

While at St. Mike's, I met John McCauley, whose son, Wes, played on the team. Mr. McCauley knew hockey and always had a positive outlook. An NHL referee, he rose to be the NHL director of officiating. He gave me pointers and showed me the ropes of how to protect myself on the ice. He advised my parents on the pitfalls of amateur and pro hockey. Our families became close friends. Their family still spends Christmas Eve with us.

Shockingly, Mr. McCauley died of complications during a routine operation at age forty-four. I was sixteen years old. It crushed me. I used to wear number 8 before I met Mr. McCauley, who also wore the same number. When I joined the Oshawa Generals, someone already had number 8, so I decided to put my number and Mr. McCauley's side by side for number 88. That's been my number ever since as tribute to my favorite NHL official.

Once I made it to the NHL, I got the chance to play alongside my heroes, like Mark Messier.

On my sixteenth birthday, I received a wonderful surprise. Mr. McCauley told Mark Messier, my favorite player, that it was my birthday. Mark kindly signed a hockey stick to me. I slept with that stick beside my bed for months. It's still in my old bedroom.

When I turned sixteen, I became eligible for the Ontario Hockey League draft. We were told I could be among the top players picked, so we thought about my options. Sault Ste. Marie, almost 400 miles away from Toronto, picked me first overall.

My parents were concerned about the nine-hour drive and the disruption it would cause in our family to travel that far to watch me play. Mostly, they were concerned about my education. Before the draft, the team's academic advisor told us I would not be able to finish high school on time due to the team's extensive travel schedule. That was unacceptable. My parents insisted I finish high school before turning pro. Even with my man-sized body, emotionally I was still just sixteen and didn't feel ready to live that far away from my family either.

So we respectfully expressed our concerns. They refused to listen to me as a person. I had nothing against the city, its people, or the team. It just wasn't a good fit. After Sault Ste. Marie drafted me anyway, I refused to report. League rules didn't allow trades.

An opportunity arose for me to continue my high school education in Detroit and play for the University of Michigan in January. I had been accepted to UM based on my test scores, but I needed to finish high school first. To do that, I went to summer school in Detroit to graduate early. While I attended high school, I played in the United States Junior Hockey League. I lived with a great family, the Velluccis, near Detroit, Michigan, about a three-hour drive from Toronto.

It took me a little while to adjust to my adopted family, whom I had never met. My first day I freaked out. After I arrived, Judy Vellucci, the mother, left me home alone while she ran errands. I remembered hearing something about riots in Detroit a long time ago and became frightened that someone might try to break in.

I locked myself in the bathroom until Judy came back home. I flushed the toilet over and over and counted tiles in the room to pass the time. I can laugh about it now. I had no reason to feel unsafe, but I had this unfounded fear and I was afraid to say anything about it.

It didn't take long to relax and feel at home. Judy made the mistake of telling me to eat whatever I wanted, so I did.

I made myself comfortable in my room by allowing

it to resemble my room at my parents' house—messy.

Sports Illustrated did a feature story on me in Detroit and took this picture of my room. Brett is the opposite when it comes to clutter. When we shared a

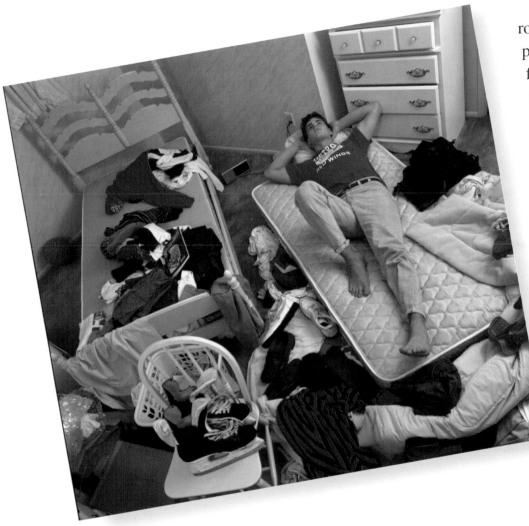

room, his half would be perfectly in place, and mine would be a disaster. In fact, we divided our room with white floor tape so I wouldn't mess up his side.

My stay in Detroit lasted eight months. I graduated from high school in Michigan in January, thanks to my receiving extra credits from three years of summer courses. The extra work gave me options. But I never attended the University of Michigan. I played in just fourteen USHL games, scoring fifty-two points (twenty-three goals).

That's because the OHL decided to change its no-trade rule, allowing Sault Ste. Marie to trade my rights to the Oshawa Generals. Oshawa is a comfortable forty-five-minute drive from Toronto, so I finished the season with the Generals.

I remember during the Memorial Cup, Eric drove back to Toronto on the weeknights so he wouldn't miss his classes at York University.
—Colleen Corner, Oshawa Generals office manager

1990–91 Season
OHL scoring champion
OHL's Most Valuable Player
Hockey News Junior Player of the Year
Sixteen game-winning goals—an OHL record

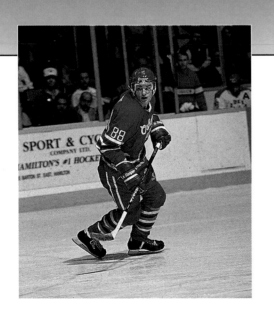

That season we won the Memorial Cup, the championship for Major Junior Hockey. It was Oshawa's first Cup in forty-six years. The whole city went nuts.

I played the entire 1990–91 season in Oshawa. I lived with a new family, but drove back to Toronto several days a week to start classes at York University.

The players all dedicated much of their lives to hockey and had big dreams of playing in the NHL. Those were exciting times. You never knew which NHL scouts were in the stands watching.

Hockey at that amateur level, in some ways, is rougher than the NHL. The long bus rides (sometimes ten hours one way) combined with school the next day can wear you down. Playing with the Generals prepared me for being a professional. I remember we had a sign in the Oshawa locker room that read: "The willingness to win is not as important as the willingness to prepare."

That summer, my dream of playing in the NHL became a nightmare. The Nordiques—then located in Quebec City, Quebec, before moving to Denver in 1995—had the worst record. Curiously, they had the first draft pick, despite one expansion team's coming into the league.

The NHL has the most restrictive rules in pro sports regarding free agency. That meant the team I first signed with could lock me up for most of my career because I wouldn't be eligible for unrestricted free agency until I turned thirty-two.

We studied the situation as a family but I decided that the Nordiques were not a team I wanted to join. Just like Sault Ste. Marie, I had nothing against French-speaking Quebec or its people. It wasn't about money. I wasn't trying to stand up to the league. I had a problem with the owner, how he treated players, and his lack of commitment to winning.

We met team officials before the draft and asked them not to pick me, or to at least work out a trade. But on draft day, sure enough, the Nordiques made me the 1991 first pick overall.

I put on a strong face that day for pictures and media interviews. Inside I crumbled, knowing that this was going to be a long, ugly fight. After the draft, Brett and I got into a cab. I collapsed onto him and let my emotions, and tears, flow. When my willingness to sit out the season became clear, the Nordiques turned up the heat and tried to turn all of Canada against me.

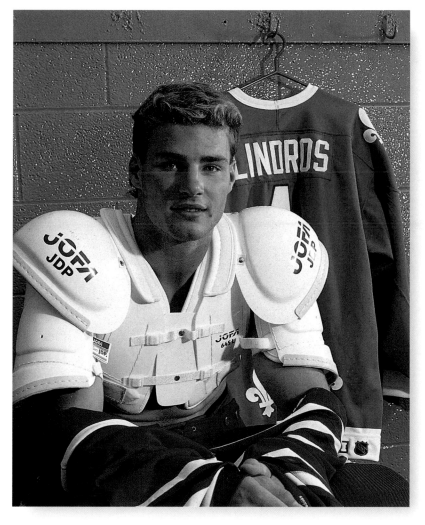

Who was I to defy the NHL? they asked. They called me a spoiled baby. They called my mother worse things. I felt the pressure from all sides, but I was willing to protect the pursuit of my goals no matter what. I still had my freedom of choice.

I spent part of the next season (1991–92) with the Generals and the rest representing Canada. I played on the Canada Cup team and the Olympic team, all in the same season.

Being on the Canada Cup team, with the top NHL pros, thrilled and chilled me. Playing at age 18 against the world's best, including my childhood heroes, made me uneasy at first. I felt awed.

I found out soon enough they weren't gods. "I can play with these guys," I told myself after the first practice.

Our Canada Cup team also won the tournament. My confidence soared being around those pro players and asking them questions about how I could prepare myself for the NHL. I've never been afraid to talk with people and dig for the golden nuggets of their experience. If you know where you want to go, ask those who have been there for directions.

Brett and me.

Before I turned pro, I played in the ultimate national experience—the Olympic Games.

The 1992 Winter Games at Albertville, France, lifted my spirits at the right time. The grind of hearing about my NHL situation over and over had me down. Then, for a magical month, I felt part of something big, something that unified Canada. None of our top NHL countrymen were on our team. We had some current and former NHLers, but we were mostly a group of kids who played well together.

Before the tournament, we relaxed by sliding down groomed ski slopes at night on cafeteria trays. I made sure I didn't run into snow banks this time. Just seeing players trying to fit onto the trays made everyone laugh.

Tensions mounted quickly for us in the quarterfinals as our game

In the 1998 Nagano Games, I was honored to be selected captain of the Canadian Olympic team.

with Germany went to a shootout, the first in Olympic hockey history.

I took the first of five shots for our team. I missed, just over the net. I felt as if I had let down our whole country. I sat by myself and watched as a 2-2 shootout tie sent us into a sudden-death shootout for the game-winner. I got another chance. This time I scored with a hard drive to the right, a head fake, and a low screamer into the net.

All of Canada seemed to support us. One day we got 31,000 letters from schoolchildren back home. In the gold medal game, we faced the Russians (then called the Unified Team) and lost 3-1. As competitors we wanted the gold, but the pain didn't last too long as we realized that our silver medal was the first Olympic hockey medal for Canada in twenty-four years, and the first silver in thirty-two years.

More than a year passed before the Nordiques finally traded me. The owner showed his true colors by trading me to two teams at the same time. It took a third party to figure out that the Philadelphia Flyers could complete a trade that sent six players, two first-round draft picks, and $15 million (U.S.) to Quebec for me. After competing with and against many who played for the Nordiques and hearing more about their situation, I'm glad things worked out the way they did.

Naturally, I wanted to prove myself in my rookie season. For the most part, I think I did, scoring forty-one goals in sixty-one games. I enjoy playing in Philadelphia. The Flyer fans can be tough because they know hockey. They appreciate players who give everything they have, and that's what I try to do every night.

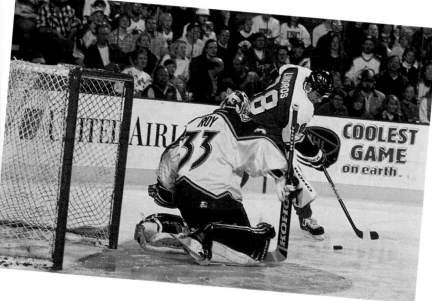

A character test for me came that first year when we played in Quebec. Nordique fans let fly verbal attacks. Many wore diapers on their heads and waved pacifiers at me, calling me a baby.

My feeling is that when fans pay for a ticket, they can say what they want about me. Fans cursed at me. Others spit. Some threw food and drinks.

It's never easy to take that abuse. Hockey players are not robots. But it comes with the territory. As long as fans don't throw things on the ice, which could hurt a player, I've learned to take it.

Everyone is faced with confrontations. The trick is being wise enough to know how to react—should you stand up to it, back off, or stand there and take it. Most of the time I make the right decision.

To be a balanced person, I need other interests outside of hockey. Fishing is one of my favorite hobbies. During the summer, I enjoy waterskiing and golfing. I go out bowling sometimes, but I'm a terrible bowler.

Brett had it tougher then me coming up through the hockey ranks. Many took physical and mental shots at him. "You're not as good as your older brother," they would say.

Brett endured and became a first-round pick of the New York Islanders in 1994. We never played in the same age level before, so the first time we shared the same ice came during an NHL game. It felt strange yet familiar at the same time. Although we played countless games on our backyard rink, we only played against each other a handful of times in the NHL.

We bumped into each other a few times during those games and loved every collision.

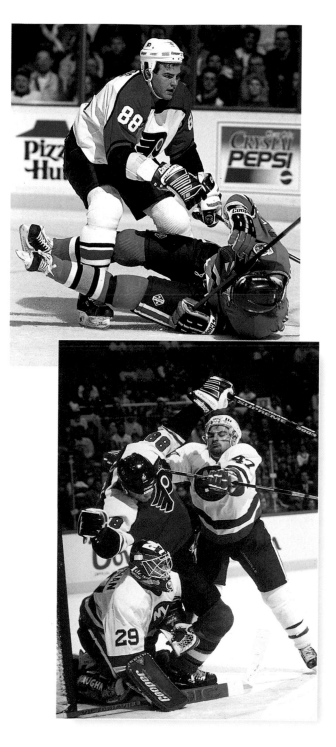

Everyone knows hockey is a rough sport. The physical contact is one aspect that makes hockey fun to play and watch. Just like a football player who makes an aggressive tackle, I get a charge from making a big hit on the ice.

Don't get me wrong. I don't ever try to intentionally injure anyone, and I don't take pleasure in seeing other players in pain.

Being a big guy, I'm a big target, and I've taken my share of hits, too.

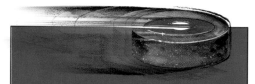

I think people have the wrong impression. He hits hard and plays a tough game, but he cares about other people. Last year he knocked a guy out, and Eric was shaken. Nobody wants to go around and hurt anyone.
–John LeClair, Flyer teammate

Where there's contact, there are sports injuries, and I've had my share through the years. The speed and ice-hard rink surroundings put hockey players at risk.

The most dangerous injury in any sport is to the head. Even the best helmets can't prevent the most common head injury—a concussion.

Have you ever shaken a bowl of Jell-O? That's what happens to your brain when your head hits something hard. Your brain wiggles and bangs against your skull.

A concussion can be minor, leaving you dazed or dizzy. That's sometimes called "having your bell rung." Serious concussions can cause loss of memory, loss of consciousness, or worse.

WHAT IS A CONCUSSION?

A change in mental status from a whiplash of the neck or direct blow to the head, face, or jaw.

Grades of concussions

Grade 1

1. Temporary confusion or inability to carry out goal-directed movements.
2. No loss of consciousness.
3. Dizziness, headaches, nausea, lethargy, may have some memory loss.
4. Concussion symptoms or mental status abnormalities resolve in less than 15 minutes.

Grade 2

Same as Grade 1 except symptoms last longer than 15 minutes.

Grade 3

Any loss of consciousness.

What to do after first concussion

Grade 1

1. Remove from contest.
2. Examine immediately and at five-minute intervals for the development of mental status abnormalities or post-concussive symptoms at rest or with exertion.
3. Always check for neck injury.
4. Should not return to play without approval of physician and at least twenty-four hours rest.

Grade 2

Same as Grade 1, plus physician should perform a neurological exam to clear the athlete for return to play after one full week without symptoms at rest and with exertion.

Grade 3

1. Transport athlete from field to nearest emergency department by ambulance if still unconscious or if worrisome signs are detected (with cervical spine immobilization if indicated).
2. A thorough neurological evaluation should be performed immediately, including appropriate neuroimaging procedures when indicated.
3. Hospital admission is advised if the mental status remains abnormal.
4. A physician should clear athlete for return to play after at least one week of symptom-free rest for unconsciousness of less than one minute; and two weeks rest for unconsciousness of more than a minute and less than five minutes.

My family, including my sister Robin, who is my biggest fan.

Any concussion is a serious matter. Brett discovered that in 1995. Players who have one concussion are at risk for greater damage should they have a second shortly after the first. Concussions year after year also put athletes at greater risk.

Brett suffered several concussions before his second pro season. However, that second year he had back-to-back concussions within a week. They caused headaches and an inability to concentrate, to drive a car, and even to dial a phone. These and other strange things lasted for weeks.

Doctors told him another concussion could cause permanent brain damage. So at the beginning of his pro hockey career, Brett walked away from the game.

I'm proud of my brother as a player, but I'm even more impressed with how he has bounced back from his misfortune and adjusted his goals. He's still in the game as the television host of a show featuring NHL players, called "Be A Player."

As a family, we decided to turn Brett's experience into something positive. We helped raise awareness and money to provide information about concussions. A special card outlining accepted medical information about concussions was printed and given to hockey leagues throughout Canada. It gave coaches and parents the facts about the warning signs and guidelines for concussions. The same information is printed on these two pages.

Thanks to the cards, more people know about the need for an appropriate rest period after a concussion.

One off-the-ice activity that's been rewarding for me is working with the Children's Miracle Network. The organization raises money for children treated in 170 hospitals throughout North America.

I lend a hand by going to hospitals to meet young patients and helping them raise money through telethons and charity events. I think I get more out of it than the kids.

So often it's easy to get consumed by our own pursuit that we forget to reach out and help others with theirs.

What to do after second or more concussions

- For second Grade 1 or 2 concussions, consider terminating the season, but there should be a minimum of one month's rest and a physician should clear the athlete for return to play only after one week free of symptoms.
- For second Grade 3 concussion, terminate the season; may return next season with approval of attending physician.
- For a third concussion of any grade, terminate the season.

Warning signs

Vacant stares (befuddled facial expressions); delayed verbal and motor responses (slow to answer questions or follow instructions); confusion and inability to focus attention (easily distracted and unable to follow through with normal activities); disorientation (walking in wrong direction, unaware of time, date, and space); slurred or incoherent speech (making disjointed or incomprehensible statements); gross observable incoordination (stumbling, inability to walk tandem/straight line); emotions out of proportion to circumstance (distraught, crying for no apparent reason); memory deficits (exhibited by the athlete repeatedly asking the same question that has already been answered, or inability to memorize 3 of 3 words or 3 of 3 objects in 5 minutes); headaches; dizziness, nausea, blurred, or double vision; any period of loss of consciousness.

Do not attempt to treat a concussion. Always consult a physician!

These guidelines were approved by the Canadian Brain Injury Coalition and the Canadian Hockey Association in November of 1997.

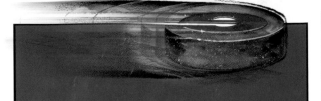

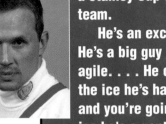

After we beat the Flyers in the Stanley Cup, I told Eric, "Don't beat yourself up." . . . One person can't make a team a winner. I haven't seen one superstar win a Stanley Cup without a supporting team.

He's an excellent all-around player. He's a big guy who is mobile and agile. . . . He can dominate a game. On the ice he's hard—he's going to hit you and you're going to feel it—but off the ice he's a gentleman.

—Steve Yzerman, Detroit Red Wings

He's always telling jokes. He likes to keep things really loose. We were getting ready for the Olympics in Japan and he set up a mock TV interview with Japanese reporters. He got me to dress up in a kimono, and it was all a joke.

–John LeClair, Flyer teammate

I played my last NHL game against Eric. After the game, I whispered in his ear, "Now it's your time. Now it's time for you and Jaromir Jagr to take over the game."

—Mario Lemieux

The goal of all NHL teams at the start of the season is to win the Stanley Cup trophy. We missed the playoffs my first two seasons in Philly and then made respectable post-season showings the next two years.

I experienced my first taste of the NHL Finals in 1997 when we met the Detroit Red Wings. Philadelphia had waited 10 years since its last trip to the finals. Disappointingly, we were no match for the Red Wing machine, losing four straight games. Detroit kept me boxed up all series.

I took the defeat hard. It took me the whole summer to get over it. Red Wings captain Steve Yzerman has a summer lake cabin close to mine. Long talks with Steve helped shake off my depression. I have long respected him as a player and a person. He has encouraged me throughout my career.

During the '92 Olympics, I cleared a puck resting on the back of the goal net by reaching through the front end of the goal and banging the mesh with my stick to free the puck. Then I raced back around to get the puck and took another shot on goal.

Whatever the team standings, every athlete must have a tremendous drive to win. When you lose that, you shouldn't play competitive sports anymore. But I believe the pursuit of your goals should be enjoyable as well. You have to enjoy the ride and laugh a little.

One thing I love about hockey is how creative you can be. Hockey is not just about brute strength. When I'm trying to beat someone with the puck, I can't make the same move over and over. I have to change and continue to create new moves. That keeps the game interesting. There is always something new to learn.

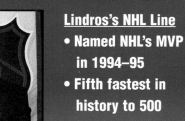

Lindros's NHL Line
• Named NHL's MVP in 1994–95
• Fifth fastest in history to 500 career points
• Five-time NHL All-Star selection

On Oct. 1, 1999, I returned to the NHL ice for the first time since my lung injury.

As long as I play in the NHL, I will pursue the goal of winning a Stanley Cup.

Whatever your goals, be more than a dreamer; be a doer. Believe in yourself. Trust yourself to try.

Because in the end, attaining all of your goals is not as important as pursuing your goals.